anythink

How Small Is a Hummingbird?

The Child's World®

childsworld.com

Published by The Child's World®
1980 Lookout Drive • Mankato, MN 56003-1705
800-599-READ • www.childsworld.com

Photographs ©: Glass and Nature/Shutterstock Images, cover, 1, 8–9; SumikoPhoto/iStockphoto, 2–3; Shutterstock Images, 4, 4–5, 6–7, 10–11 (top), 12, 14–15; Andrey Lobachev/Shutterstock Images, 7; Steve Byland/Shutterstock Images, 10–11 (bottom); Martin Mecnarowski/Shutterstock Images, 12–13; FloridaStock/Shutterstock Images, 16–17; Keneva Photography/Shutterstock Images, 18–19; Karel Cerny/Shutterstock Images, 20–21; Sergio Hayashi/Shutterstock Images, 23

ISBN 9781503816800
LCCN 2016945667

Printed in the United States of America
PA02325

ABOUT THE AUTHOR

Kurt Waldendorf is a writer and editor. He lives in Vermont with his wife and their Old English sheepdog, Charlie.

NOTE FOR PARENTS AND TEACHERS

The Child's World® helps early readers develop their informational-reading skills by providing easy-to-read books that fascinate them and hold their interest. Encourage new readers by following these simple ideas:

BEFORE READING

- Page briefly through the book. Discuss the photos. What does the reader think he or she will learn in this book? Let the child ask questions.
- Look at the glossary together. Discuss the words.

READ THE BOOK

- Now read the book together, or let the child read the book independently.

AFTER READING

- Urge the child to think more. Ask questions such as, "What things are different among the animals shown in this book?"

A hummingbird is the smallest type of bird. How small is a hummingbird?

3

A hummingbird
hatches from an egg.
Each egg is the size of
a coffee bean.

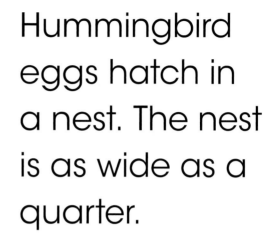

Hummingbird eggs hatch in a nest. The nest is as wide as a quarter.

Hummingbirds drink **nectar** from flowers. A hummingbird grows to be as long as a key.

Some **insects** are similar in size to hummingbirds. A hummingbird is the length of two bumblebees.

Hummingbirds do not weigh much. An adult hummingbird weighs as much as a dime.

A robin is a small **songbird**.
It weighs as much as five
hummingbirds.

A hummingbird is so small that it does not have many feathers. An eagle has seven times more feathers than a hummingbird.

A hummingbird's **wingspan** is the length of a crayon. A hummingbird beats its wings 80 times every second.

At night, a hummingbird finds a safe place to rest. It can rest on something as small as a pencil eraser.

CHECK IT OUT!

▶ There are hundreds of types of hummingbirds. The smallest is the bee hummingbird.

▶ Hummingbirds are known for their bright colors.

▶ A hummingbird's heart beats more than 1,000 times each minute.

▶ Hummingbirds use their tongues to drink. They can lick 13 times in one second.

▶ Hummingbirds have tiny feet. Hummingbirds' feet are so weak they cannot walk.

GLOSSARY

insects (IN-sekts) Insects are small animals with wings, three pairs of legs, and no backbones. Some insects are similar in size to hummingbirds.

nectar (NEK-tur) Nectar is a sweet liquid from flowers. Hummingbirds hover in front of plants and drink their nectar.

songbird (SAWNG-burd) A songbird is a bird that has a musical call. A robin is a small songbird.

wingspan (WING-span) A bird's wingspan is the distance from the tip of one wing to the other. A hummingbird's wingspan is shorter than any other bird's.

TO LEARN MORE

BOOKS

Gregory, Josh. *Hummingbirds*.
New York, NY: Children's Press, 2017.

Kenney, Karen Latchana. *Tiny Animals*.
Mankato, MN: Amicus, 2011.

Spilsbury, Louise. *Superstar Birds*.
New York, NY: PowerKids Press, 2015.

WEB SITES

Visit our Web site for links about hummingbirds:
childsworld.com/links

Note to Parents, Teachers, and Librarians: We routinely verify our Web links to make sure they are safe and active sites. So encourage your readers to check them out!

INDEX